WAITING UP FOR
THE END
OF THE WORLD

conspiracies

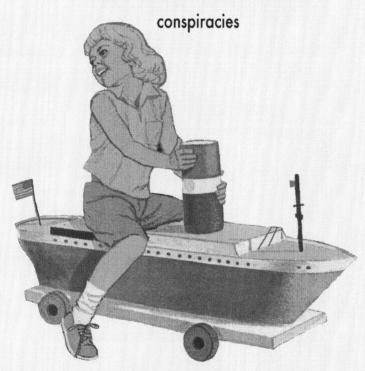

elizabeth j. colen

art by Guy Benjamin Brookshire

WAITING UP FOR
THE END
OF THE WORLD

(CONSPIRACIES)

Elizabeth J. Colen

Jaded Ibis Press
sustainable literature by digital means™
an imprint of Jaded Ibis Productions U.S.A.

COPYRIGHTED MATERIAL

© 2012 copyright Elizabeth J. Colen

ISBN: 978-1-937543-14-3

Library of Congress Control Number: 2012939088

Printed in the United States of America. No part of this book may be used or reproduced in any manner whatsoever without written permission from the publisher, except in the case of brief quotations embodied in critical articles and reviews. For information please email: questions@jadedibisproductions.com

Published by Jaded Ibis Press, sustainable literature by digital means™ An imprint of Jaded Ibis Productions, LLC, Seattle, Washington USA   http://jadedibisproductions.com

Cover art by Guy Brookshire.

〇

(CONTENTS)

(ASSASSINATION INTERLUDE)

(2)

(1)

(0)

And the autumn fruit your soul longed for
  has gone from you,
and all the luxurious and the brilliant
  are lost to you
  and never will be found.

—John of Patmos

I bury the dead in my belly.

–Arthur Rimbaud

JUST AFTER TAKEOFF

In losing the landing gear we give up the rhythm a little.
There is a thump, the lights dim and go out.

What have we learned? Disaster will strike. The East River is no warmer
than the Hudson. Birds have it in for us. The sky remains blue, even after.

They will allow profanity on the news, but only on occasion. The wind will whip
with feathers and no one will go on talking except the man at the front of the plane.

The black box records in silence.

The triple-proof of our love: I didn't say anything to you. You said nothing to me.
And neither of us spoke to God.

This is how I loved you t-minus whatever, one hand on your thigh,
one hand covering the back of my head.

(4)

FLUORIDE IS FLUORESCENT INCANDESCENT

There's a man who can only tell his wife by her dentist.
White coat checks incisors and decides it's her, the right wife;
they go on for another year, tucked into a ranch-style
with no horses, no cowboy anything,
just handfuls of brief stairs and long spans of shag carpet.

We let the tap run, never minding water conservation.
We raised the fishes with fluoride until their gills whistled,
and they grew teeth, skin became orange, then red, then dead.
Your father's lungs could not withstand the power of smokestacks
or laundry detergent, could not withstand you and your brother fighting.

If he coughed, the gig was up; it was as good as yelling.
It started in the factory. Bombs were constructed and children
with leaden smiles, paint flecks hidden
between stark white teeth didn't have to be told to behave.
They were just. That. Good.

THE DEVIL WAGES ORDINARY WARS
New World Order

Uneasy heavens await people dancing in the street,
people thinking they could get more out of the bargain than breathing is.

People in suits and street clothes ripping up the pavement in search of
pennies thrown by black-fisted flyers of burning planes.

What war did we go on to?

I touch the side of every air-bound silo,
the real cold slickshine, beg the watering can not to turn and rain its people
down.

Uneasy heavens wait for men to repaint the pearly gates,
the glare's too much in all this goodness.

We went with grey for the area we wouldn't allow
until now

when everything's the matter.

LOST LAND THEORISTS
New World Order

On a sky-blind lurch of lichen,
under perihelion,
where water waits, sonde
of piano lesson through the trees.

The teacher waits,
                            interrupts.
The child starts up again,
glissando fist under threat
of early darkness.
                    We supersede
the greys or hollow earth,
reptilian flares, the rutted railcar darkness.
In soot and hollow beam,
in psychosocial hypothesis—
                                    hypostasis.

When the train horn blows
you take my hand again, over fist, under
over; we can't get right.
                    Thistle rip
in thin skin sticks.
The child will find the key.
The undercoat of moss locks lichen to a tree.

MEN WHO RUN BACKWARDS
North American Union

We want water, wind. There are men who run backwards.
There's nothing to worry about; my father learned this in the army.

In talk of tracks, trains, and shipping lanes, it's more important to see what's left behind.
I look at the plains from the plane, brown din of desiccated fields.

My father had eyes in his hair. We don't even bend to slight degrees,
no change in elevation. Thin brow, back of the head;

he didn't run into anything. I think of deer crossing,
skunks, raccoons. Animals still on the shoulder.

Dad on the curved track at the high school, faster. His students clapping their hands,
having given up on what green looks like. Girls rolling up sleeves, tanning arms.

In the passing lane death looks like the brightest bird, a class act in fractured glass.
Here, in the lie of sun. Gum burns on crushed shells. And something sounds like thunder.

No distant train, no wind and steam through grain fields.
Jersey barrier, a raw patch. If I couldn't see it didn't matter.

Painted lines. If father didn't watch, it never happened. Painted line,
the corner cracking. The bleacher's knotted railing. I slipped right through.

TOSHIBA BOMBEAT
Pan Am Flight 103

I watched the girl's body breathe between bits of her bikini. Something in me shriveled. I didn't know her eyes were closed. This was not the day we learned what death was. We played tetherball until someone wrecked my brother's eye into a blood blister that would grow all day. We couldn't take his crying. At noon and two, the captain threw strange coins from foreign lands into the deep end. Lungs full of wasted air, hand around some pfennig, dinar, escudo, centavo, I paused each time, drifting at the bottom to see what a mess the sky was.

SOCIOLOGY OF MYTHMAKING

Area 51

We keep looking
up for someone else.
I had a name for this.
Fission, the force of will
molded moans and half-
words into facts.
Stand aside for reason.
No one wants to know
how air collides with air
and where what doesn't fit gets in.

Between claps of thunder, mind like a silver
wing, like a six-sided thought taking wind.

What's hidden, truth
dons an oblong mask,
peeks through wet black holes.
On TV we watch a marathon: *War of the Worlds,*
Invasion of the Body Snatchers, War of the Worlds,
the updated version.

This is what our lives are like. This is where we come from.
You don't believe in expectations; I don't believe in paper trails.

The TV sizzles into a small, blind spark.
I take a forty-five minute shower in water I don't have to pay for.

We'll sleep like sullen coffins, emptied of the dead.
And when the stars align, I'll kiss you. It's true we're dust of them.

REGOLITH AND SILICA
Lunar Landing

Men on the moon put thin
wires in the flag to make it look blown
by wind, but why?
In Bend, your head's tossed back
looking at the black night around us
so spotted with distant suns we'll never have names for.

Pale purple glow of town
a few miles off reminds us
we're taking up space.
Streaks light the sky,
but we stopped wishing after the seventh shooting star.
What more could we hope for?

The lie of a man in a suit,
the C on a rock, cross-
hair fiducials. "Do you think it's true?"
you ask and I don't know which way you mean.
"That it happened or didn't," I say. And you say yes,
so I say nothing.

Una Ronald said she saw an astronaut
kick a pop bottle. Did it settle
in silicon dust, lost to Houston's six-second delay?
We drink beers out of cans and think about the moon's dark,
absent of stars.

THE NURSE HAS NEVER BEEN FOUND

Area 51

A boy stands on a cloudbank,
caught in a comic book snare.

We're in No Name, New Mexico,
taunted by big eyes, opaline.

Batlike wings over Chehalis, over Rainier.

Pie plate, radiosonde between
tumbleweeds, balsawood hieroglyphics.

Boy's father enters the room.
Metal folded unfolds. Nothing burns.

Nurse draws concentric circles for the undertaker.
The nurse has never been found.

No one heard the word of God, but they believed.
No one saw the boneset,

gumboil, the appetite, thrum,
balloon of bodies.

SELF-CONTAINED SELF-RESCUE DEVICE

Peak Oil

Combustion. Sand. Still there's no bounce to the trigger.
Hair on end in hand-hammered pockets of methane.

You can't stop progress. The grass is fine on the other side.
Though green or greener, limed. Finer than mines casting out slack.

Prognostic sigh sparks a light, mile-high sulfur in downwind.
Progress is slow now, word is the wonder.

Hand to the wall, notch etches a palm.
Nicks in the rock reckoned into numbers you'll know.

Memorize dates of strangers. Birthdays and when you met.
The love, and when it got used up.

Engine leads engine to another machine.
Waiting on the train, wheel, or jig concentrator,

we swear by plants and warm-blooded animals, swear by sequined stun-guns,
draglines left loose in Davy lamps, our right hands to cog.

CARLOS ALIEN VS. THE U.S. NAVY
The Philadelphia Experiment

Amidst the green fog, flash of light,
amidst the stopped-watch handme-
down. Paid forward from two days behind.
What went down in Philly went down in Virginia,
went down in Philly, lost at the end of the war.

Lost days lost at the end of the war.
By the blue book the lights went down.
One more shock from Pennsylvania, one more shock
devoured water, where Lindberg's baby was lost,
was found. It's not too late.

We went where the water boiled
beneath the yellow headlights
of fighter planes. Men attached
to hulls pulled at legs that weren't there,
arms that weren't there.

                    Whole halves of themselves
married to the ship,
buried in the mess of time aligning.

YAHODIE

The Philadelphia Experiment

The ship thumps twice against the wave, then quiets. We're docked, but weather warns
in stitches to the back of a stumbling sailor's head. *He hasn't got his sealegs yet.*

Project Yahodie, alien spies, UFO darling touts teleportation.
Fourteen men got stuck starboard, attached when—one bit through his wrist to get free.

They said Lost at Sea, but we were docked. They said drop your watches in the pail
as you enter, something about magnetics. Nothing about the true time.

Man said *degaussing* and we thought funeral pyre, but we were brave for the rest of them.
Smoke lifting. Hiss listening. Second hand spinning like mad.

They say Einstein made us up, then forgot or fought us.
They say a ship can be a graveyard.

Head in stone, body flopping against steel,
against the green fog lifting. Hold on to something.

The ship thumps twice in Philly. Lights dim,
and then flicker. Lights dim, and then go out.

AMERICAN FEAR
9/11

Understand,
shadow is the echo of vision.

What comes first and last must meet at building's edge.
A pencil through a screen.

There's a man in the station giving out hair,
clumps he's ripped from women.

This is what we wanted:
the TV's on; we're in it.

Ghost in the voicemail memorizing lines.
Red hair with your mouth on fire.

Standing in the hall with your jacket
tight around you,

fear the outside getting in—
hand to hot door.

SEVENTEEN MILES
Fluoride

I once walked backwards for seventeen miles.
My comb got lost on the history of your hair,

and I forgot where I put you.
Teeth shine. Water in my water.

Teeth with tiger stripes, cheetah spots.
Top the flossing with an animal grin.

What little there was between us in the first three days
was reduced to toothpaste.

Flecks on the mirror between spots of your face.

Dry well, marked pink by morning sun, you
slathered in you.

You *loved* me.

There's a cat in my basement filled with Diazepam,
my bottle of pills. Wheezy pads on concrete—

what wonder, this seizure.

CALIFORNIA ICE AGE
                    HAARP

1.

You stand under the eaves.
I'll watch from the house,
pit dark in the pitch black, my legs muddied from rain.

I have only what I brought in my pockets.
It is the square rock that soothes me.
The wonder of how the corners were hewed.

And when we depart, wings of the rest of us—
shared brown eyes blown clear green—
when we depart, sounds of the neighborhood

join sounds from our insides. Fear builds
a stomach symphony about fire in the desert.
Hands up.

And feet given up.
Hands up, shout louder in your language.
It doesn't mean a thing.

2.

Black wet confluence of history=small girl meets

block after block of Family Lives Lie and Calls it Hope.
There's the torrent, then the ionized children we knew
we were, glowing in the underbrush, clutching at stars.

Scratching green letters onto pavement thick
with blown leaves.

Brother lover,
we remember.

3.

A=candy cane. B=mud on the stairs. C=black leather suitcase.
The space where it was on the floor absent of dust.

4.

Treetops look like mountain ridges, sway.
A harsh sound. *Temblor,* I say.

Tremble. The place where father lives
is governed by thieves. Where he left us.

He died/never left us.

5.

Written into skyline. And this is how we happen.
Contrails melt, evaporate lights with weather.

Red risking the water,
turning the red into blue.

GENESIS
Pearl Harbor

Nothing would become of him.
My brother once stapled a girl's arm to her sleeve.

And though once remembered
for how long he could hold his breath,

once breath stopped,
the memory was gone.

Eleanor,
red in her gown.

In the quarry pit he sank into a hole.
The bleeding was simple.

The minutes ticked and we were with him.
Red was on roses, blue barrette in her hair.

There are no screams under water.
But she didn't want him.

There is nothing to hold onto that looks like us.
There is only green. And what's left in your lungs.

HOME BEFORE DARK, THE PROTOCOLS OF

The Protocols of Zion

The boy I was then stood on a dirt hill miles from anything. He proclaimed to own it all. Ants climbed his legs and he let them. They died in a V on his jeans, covered in poison stolen from an unlocked shed. Two dirt clods shook boy me into stumbling.

No one owns me.

Because my name can be spelled wrong, I can be held down too. The protocol of things learned quickly. Face to the mound. They searched for horns in my hair.

When we were eleven we made slaves of the girls next door. No one knew how we made them be.

Twenty-four doors slam shut in twenty-four houses. Twenty-four laws. When we were young we could fit three rules on our hands. *Don't show fear. Give away nothing. Home before dark.*

(3)

KING HUBBERT
Peak Oil

Inside,
the earth's
core
is hollow.
Inside
the hollow
is a tiny
beating
heart named
Sludge.

We dredge her.

Minute
by minute
there are
men shaking
fists, men
losing lives,
wires down
with mud
bricks,
clay.

It's bone, love.
We saw it
shaped
this way.
How we

wonder. And
two by three
the core of this
shakes, diamond-
tipped.

What was it
you wanted to say?

It isn't right
that it's so
easy. Well-
mannered
thieves under
manicured eaves.
Flesh-colored scars
mar the surface.
Google earth
leaves us dry.

From this
we're calm.
We know that under
every dollar is another
            dollar.

Under every hundred,
another hundred
burns. Of sun
another sun
another sun another
sun.

END OF THE WORLD

Barrel on
barrel,
this
is how
the west
was earned.

MOTOR OF THE WORLD
North American Union

Tell me you're in trouble, I'll find a machine that fits that.
Like a watch tick, like the memory of,
like the storm, worm or substance.

Like the grease you fielded me in.
Fold me over your fold.
Lift me over your year.

I'll be the next.
Tell me in text, dear. Tell me you're—

Tell me your sign, then.
Tell me you're fine, I mean mine,
love.

I drew so many new words.
I didn't have time for a line.

NATURAL BORN
Birthers

The ocean's wide and you were born on it. Islands, small. Even though land, was it this land, ours? If a man rakes leaves in sand—but there are no leaves. If a man rakes sand. What then? Eye to the sky; doctor's hand on a certificate. I don't believe in short forms. What do you believe in? Mother used to say, "take a long walk off a short pier," "go play in traffic." Were you born under your father's horn in Africa? Were you even your mother's child? We do math on skin tone here. Are you real enough? Are you mine? Are you with me, black man? Are you black? Are you red? Are you green? We know you're not white. Yes, speak of the blues. Sky we're under, all the waves and the news. Speak of the islands you've lived on. Talk like you've nothing to lose.

NEVADA HIGH DESERT
Lunar Landing

My boyfriend from high school called me Orion.
Bruise dark on my arm faded green after 900 hours.

What slays you will also build bloodrise to bloodrise
until, starshot, you remember names

they gave paint cans and oilrigs,
leaden-lined silos that are *supposed* to erupt into flames.

Tighten the belt, sharpen the shards.
When he read the stars, lines on our face made an A, made a C.

We were cosmic giants when he let me be.
He let me be.

Stock phrases, no flag waving, no stars and no air.
Cassiopeia, then Libra. It was harder when he looked at me.

Now 33, he wears a war he never went to;
says, "some relationships should be called in."

He stopped the car and it scarred.
Dropped the gun, shot two toes instead of one.

Second shot ripped
through another man's side.

That he settled the room without me didn't mean I had to stay.
But I had to stay. No dust on lunar lander, clean sheets—

the how I can believe him. There was that sway and swagger,
haggle, days without drink. The sun set—

I thought he did it. The sun came up;
he did it again. And then came you, so moonlight luna,

you mistake of air. I had a mind to tell you, had a way
with my words. I had a body to love you, away with my words.

It's absurd to find the flat of your stomach on every table.
Hotel room or back room, black room, the TV's always on.

The static, the empty more, trees cleaned of leaves,
that dark ocean between us, dark ocean washed over the shore.

RING OF FIRE
December 2004 Tsunami

Obfuscate the memory
before it fully settles in.

We breathe, bodies like land,
hum of plate tectonics—

earthquake in every exhalation.

*

Here a child was born—
bleached belly to a pale white sky.

No water in the eaves.
And no shade.

No eaves.

*

Over there, there are men getting ready
for someone's wedding, whittling sticks into kites.

The wife will bring lightness and upthrust.
The children will build castles

out of luck and fallen brick.

WISE MEN POISONED THE WELL
                    The Protocols of Zion

You want something solid.
The hanger in your dress puffing

up sleeves. Banner of radiation
or thieves, stopped by God,

the clicking on some machine,
A/C humming in a cramped room.

You were a girl once standing in the shadow of trees.
Your grandfather was a gun to a white man's head.

Wet leaves fell as birds scattered from the shot.
The man ran; grandpa said, *the second won't miss.*

Pale on your back in the black lake at the start of summer.
Father counting bills and mother crying in the reeds.

That night father puts a sack over mother's head,
laughs when she hits the wall running.

The dog spins in play.
By the end of summer everyone burns.

MK-NAOMI
  MK-ULTRA

Grandfather could never get his head wet.
The gas of red motion, the laboratory accident.
One night I dropped
acid in my basement room.
Grandfather on the shore,
hand over nose, blood pouring from it.
For an hour I listened to the drip of
water from the eaves.
Legs white
in winter; leg-white summer.
I watched a blast hole fan
out from the sides of my room.
Wind so insistent, ears forget
ocean and grandfather stares.
I wandered gutless.
Wind so insistent,
making a mess of his hair.
I was in the back woods,
stomach pinched, eating leaves.
Grandfather in the shallows,
the ocean loved him.
The ocean loves him.

I want to believe you'll never leave.
I woke up traveling green in
sweat- and puke-soaked sheets.
We smoke and you make a joke
about holding me down.
Tie the rope tighter.

END OF THE WORLD

My legs jerk twice. Lost in the last
jump of night
Mess of my clothes wet over sand
lost in beach grass. Shard
of your hand.

ONE COULD BUY EVERYTHING
                    North American Union

This morning
the traffic on 10
sounded like a river.
Can you hear it?
you said.
And we turned
out the lights
for another round
of dreams about empire,
fiery amero shining
in the palm of your hand.

ROUNDTRIP TICKETS

7/7 London Tube Bombing

On queue, the token
is a hot rock in a steely

fist. Push through,
squall of track and we're off

in the underground. Every face waits.
Every bag has the capacity for violence.

Bags on laps recoil with sex thoughts,
hot. We're not the ones

waiting for the world to blow.
Your hand in mine, tap your foot

heel to toe, heel to toe.
It's hard to gauge recklessness

when two trains pass.
Old man beats

fist against knee as he looks
brown face to brown face.

Summer comes from within.
A girl's necklace will strangle her.

A baby's cry
will swallow baby whole.

What we learned:
the train left the station late.

Our sources move key players track to track.
Puzzle pieces, shifting truth when truth catches up.

Man got lost on a double-
decker bus, phone call to all right,
then sky blue, sigh,
then explode.

MOBILE TETHERS
Chemtrails

Night. Salt Lake City. Blood
bruise on your lip where I hit you.

Loose shoes on the freeway.
We'd seen seventeen car crashes

since noon. All day on the highway
staring at lights, at knife stabs of chrome

when the sun shone through high clouds, haze.
Blanket of x that the planes left.

Cars with children on board, cars stuffed
with bald men smoking cigarettes,

pale arms flicking ashes out of incredibly small cars.
Cars stuffed with men. One stuffed with duds,

cowboy shirts and tambourines, black boxes of boots.
And the one we saw with blood.

Tumbleweed roadside, shoulder littered with paper,
paper hanging off trees.

You wondered if the driver was a writer.
They couldn't get him out of the car.

DEARBORN INDEPENDENT
The Protocols of Zion

Memorize wounds like highways,
like games we should win. Memorize anger,
the shape of his face, the size of his hands.

Hands become the symbol for everything.
Translate stock causes, a holy land, beat-up red Bible.
Pale cover like money, like a fist on the door.

Everything faded to white in some Russian town,
some Russian man. In some castle, some factory, store.
Mad men replicate themselves a million times over.

A million stenciled hands on the end
of stenciled arms. What we witnessed:
a red fist, a door slam. Mother empties

her purse into the front seat of the sedan.
Her best friend rides shotgun, talks about the taste
of her husband's cock.

She hates him a little less then herself.
Child rips 49 pages out of a big book before she's found
with shreds of the word, onion skin threads with saliva.

The world is just like this. Step off
the front porch into daddy's arms,
into barberry sharp like somebody's crown.

A suitcase falls open on the stairs.

The banister holds as a small woman falls.
What he meant to you:

hold steady, aim for the chin to get to the eyes.
Aim for the chest. Hand on a rack,
choosing. What we say when we lie:

aim for the chest.

THE LAWS OF MINOR STATES
                    North American Union

Do you remember any longer
what it takes to leave a room?

You stood in the hall of your father's house
while the walls were torn away.

Horse pasture sighed under smoky groans
of yellow machinery; jaws

frightened floorboards,
jaws swallowed him whole.

Life the way we meant it—
quickly. Eminent domain.

We stand in a field in Texas waiting for the rain,
cloudcover the color the concrete will be.

BÉBÉ FANTÔME, L'INDIRECT ROUTE

Princess Diana

All light along alleyways,
and halogen bulbs. Under the city,
the thirteenth pillar waits.
Like the bumper waits for
white paint scrapes, like the asphalt
for headlight parts of a Fiat.

Under the Pont de l'Alma
explosion jackknifed
like laughter—
screech and pop
of a car bending, glass shattering,
all sounds erupting at once.

What was in the report
wasn't true.
What wasn't in the van.
A man on camera
will stand up straight
no matter what's in him.

We skip the Eiffel Tower,
head straight to the tunnel,
nothing ahead of us,
nothing in rearview.
You count columns,
I slow, you say,

that one.

Pillar that killed a princess.
We're silent for her—
minds dark and damp
in the underground—
until the blood of daylight spills over again.

NOTHING IS LOST, ONLY TRANSFERRED
HAARP

The cat will only eat out of your hand,
disaster or not.

I put my fist against your chest and push hard
until you're under me,

squinting in the light in search of my eyes.

I came here for answers and stayed 49 days.
I spotted you in a bookstore downtown.

The back of your head looked like someone I had hurt once.
I held you upright and made love to you against a car.

Everyone passing knew you were asleep,
thought *we don't do that here*, but

convinced themselves your head was thrown
back in passion—

eyes closed from love.

(ASSASSINATION INTERLUDE)

THE MATHEMATICS OF

Just before your pinked
body turns, hand

raised in wave, lift
a hair up to the light.

Sun's tearing over everything anyway.
You're not blonde now, you're not born now,

you're her and you're in it, for all your pill-
box neatly atop the shine of your scalding

black as berry, black
alder hair. There's a trembling in the trees

we've not seen before. Freeze
the sky and the plane stops, mid-

way to the sun. Then sun stops,
midway through the universe. And all

the cars and all the people stop on the street below.

But what we're here to see: three bullets
stationary, four. Four bullets, stock-

still in the mathematics of our outline.
If you want to, yes we've duplicated time.

Four tiny missiles bathing in the terrible sun.

We walk around them, examine angles,
determine vectors, timing, velocity,

and the ones higher up, we have machines
for that. We can do that here. If we pluck

one hair from your head—
remember now you're Jackie—

if we pluck one hair we can do this.
Make the energy stop, the animal stop,

the man or men with the gun or guns.

Black rifle, butt against a shoulder, barrel
heat and friction, trigger

in a controlled hand.
It's part of the hand now.

We can stop the time,
but we cannot stop the killing.

When the hair falls and the time returns,
the Lincoln will be where it was, your pretty

hands, the governor's wife,
the President's head.

There is a transfer of energy.
We draw the map now.

END OF THE WORLD

The force on the bullet
will always be equal
to that on the shooter.

Bruise on the arm and the country collapses.

There will be light and there will be darkness
behind a street sign. This is where the action happens,

always off stage, just out of camera's reach.
But then we made it up.

Arms fly up like angel wings,
but he wasn't that good, was he?

A half block away, Lee sits in the lunchroom,
bottle of Coke in his hand, pretending

he knows nothing of the motorcade.
We all see him, the Coke stopped

halfway to his mouth. In that lurch of
wanting. They say the sugar did it.

Well, it was in him. Two dark
faces in the sixth-floor

window don't change the man
in the chair with the spare

change, ruddy shirt, and
affection for socialism.

Yes, that dirty word.
As good as a palm print on a rifle.

Behind the fence there may be a man
who may have a pistol aimed at

stopping John, the world, at stopping
progress. Your crawl, your lost son,

photos in every paper.

Just before your pinked body turns, so much
green, and all the sun, and then you see him,

and it's nothing you'll remember after.
Just before your body turns, white gloves, white

hand in your hair, on his arm, sun
in your eyes, smile.

Let your husband know you love him.

FROM LOVE FIELD

You stand in dust under the trees. Right where the V of fence used to be.
Some smelled smoke, some heard shots, some met the man with the dirty nails,

the fake credentials. You didn't see him get into the car. You didn't see the car.
Beyond the train tracks a man skittered down a rocky slope. By turns he slid.

Hundreds rushing to the scene, this one pushing to get out.
Frame by frame, the reel unspools. Nothing will come of it.

We saw a man once, half gallon of milk and a bag full of gulls.
He lurched and we smelled him. Some things just don't fit. The sky was so blue.

And film explains the laws of motion, which we knew once.
When you sit in the grass here, it's like we're back then,

waiting for the motorcade, the future fresh before us.

BED PARTNERS

I have nightmares of two Lees, thin lips and the stuttering. Tongue set to grab
me.
Web between forefinger and thumb saves ammo from harm.

Quiet love in the chamber. Giving out stars to the sky.
I bought one to name you.

I wasn't found in a theater in Texas. You didn't get caught running beat 78.
Three slugs at 10th and Patton felled a man, wed a man to a president. Images

flash, ragged run of the reel. Shoe man turned hero,
name on the chair of a dead man.

No one said my ears look anything like his.
Account for the hair when measuring; trichion to glabella, yes,

measure the nose, supramentale to menton, mouth opens to show teeth,
get to the ruler before the watch stop,

second hand ticks to idiot rhythms.

When we were in the back yard, when we were in Russia—hand to your hips
now—you'll never believe me. Hand to my mouth where I like it,

from that deepest depression where lower lip blocks out the sun
to the bridge of my nose until you can't hear me.

Still shots from bad cameras, static builds
over sound. Just a man hunting trouble to the sound of an engine,

Carcano rifle against Lincoln Continental. Just a mislabeled man
at the embassy. When the sun comes up Sunday,

Ruby takes it all back.

NOVEMBER 22

In the hospital where they brought him,
the governor, his wife, both wives, the pristine bullet, g-men—

on a floor wedded with wails of new lungs—
one baby was born too soon or too late.

Something was dead.
Someone said Jackie walked past her room,

but it wasn't true. Just something
to take her mind off it.

Someone said she was lucky to be alive,
but no one knew who they meant,

the one with the failed womb, dead son,
or the one riding next to a bullet,

blood on her dress and pink in her hair.

AUTOPSY IN BETHESDA

We got there long before he arrived,
Fentanyl patches and sutures, ready for pain.

We knew what he would look like
from what we'd seen on TV.

We followed the sound of the siren,
went back the way we had come.

Red against trees from rotating lights on the top of cop cars.
Against shocked wet faces, and the red of red walls.

No one had thought to draw curtains.
And there he was, or something like him.

Body soft beneath a pale yellow sheet
before they put the blackness on.

We looked to where his head would be,
but it didn't seem right.

And his feet, they didn't look like feet.
They didn't look like anything we'd seen.

NORTHWOODS

Start rumors, many. Use clandestine radio. The static will eat you and we'll start from where you fell. Wounded and twisted around those wires, red wires, green. We fought to free you. Then, seeing how warped you were and how when you opened your mouth all that came out was dull noise, we gave you a good kick and we left you.

From Havana to Miami we left you. But back in South Beach, you were sitting on a bar stool in a fresh white shirt, linen pants, with a tall glass of rum and a Cuban cigar. "I want rights to this," you said. And I nodded, which is what you should do when someone dead says anything.

Somewhere in the harbor ships were lighting up again—naphthalene. There's no point to any of this when you've seen the future. A man in uniform can stand up for forty-nine years, no matter how you kill him.

THE WOODS BEHIND GENERAL WALKER'S HOUSE

Ours was the splinter group, picking up rocks, pocketing, rocked red,
rode by on screen, on springs. Red to the one wonderland of leaves.

Our house was vacant, except for the lies mother told.
Flies ate butter off the counter. Bit by bit we stole control.

Pennies from mother's purse, dimes when we were older.
Brother folded dollars under his tongue, *dirty, tastes like paper.*

For a share we let him in on our vision of a cold-free world.
One, have friends in high places, figurative and in elevation.

Two, get a P.O. box and a name change, an alias: be somebody new.
Three, have the guts to do it all; don't mind blood or jail or pain.

Four, follow directions. Five, look surprised every time a gun
fires; wipe the powder from your hands.

TRIPLE UNDERPASS

Though we have nothing to hide
but our bed sheets and gum wrappers
and tiny bottles of gin,
we hunch like assassins in our sixth-floor hotel room.
We point the guns of our forefingers at passers-by.
A man with a striped bandana
stands south of Houston St
in the overshot of sun flicking off passing cars.

He's not playing in traffic, but yelling just to the side of it.
Is madness hereditary?
He could be my brother, blinded
by patriotism, holding to the one-bullet theory.

We the people walk to the museum,
to the library, we the people wait
for paper cuts to out our blood.
We read old news in search of names.

Old men tell us what they know.
This is not the town I grew up in.
So many businesses closing,
so many blacks in the jail.
This is the largest town without navigable water.
This is where the president came to die.

Women float like cottonwood tufts
stinking of oily perfume, hush
marks above and below crimsoned mouths.
Every lipstick here is a violence.

END OF THE WORLD

I think: all shades must lead to gunshot
or bitch slap. From the stairs I watch the crowd
reading books, pretending to read,
clicking computers.
Why does it all look so sinister?

Below me a girl watches pandas on the zoo's live cam.
I block out sounds
of someone coughing,
ear to hand, stand with waist rushing railing, like you
looking out the window on the city last night.

Now you stand at the book drop, waiting
for the next microfiche cycle to erupt
from the hands of the young boy you've befriended.
Then the hand-off, your neck gets caught in your collar,
elbows flashing up to your ears like some dance.

It would be pointless to look at you now
with so much red on your clothes.
So much of the Cape on your face.
Style of the wind, dear,
the winter wants in you.

DEAR MARINA, LOVE LEE

I have been accused of indifference, but it's not true. Sloppy sometimes looks
like an uncrossed t, undotted i. L for t makes tease look like leaves, tense
looks like lens and leave is just what it is. Across the street a nondescript house
caves in on itself; when giving directions I never mention it.

If I ran I could have killed Tippit, but I didn't. Another me from the opposite
direction. Hand on a window, hand on the butt of a gun. For candles that burn
at both ends, who holds on while twin flames reduce wax to drip and black ash?
Cuba and the U.S.S.R. The CIA, KGB, FBI, LBJ, LBJ, OSS, oh dear, my
Marina."

The boxes in the garage, stacks of old papers, doctored photos, hats that don't
fit, shoes
that you'd never wear. When I call you I'll tell you how I can't sit at a table
without taking its measure with the width of my hand. Thumb tip to pinky
stretched is the size of my heart times two, three when you're in it.

OPERATION GOOD TIMES

Thirteen body bags warmed in the open sun.
Along the cold coast boats are turning into something other than boats.

It's just as well we left our suits on under our clothes.
When we return your uncle's sprinklers will be on and we'll fasten

hands like girls, never letting go.
Along the coast, boats duck below the horizon and reappear.

There's magic there. How the brown and blue gets in. How
in '63 the plan was envy, photos of a fat man with a spread and two blonde
women.

Operation plenty, a dirty trick, man with a plan in a can in the sky.
Mercury in retrograde, or Atlas, thin hands on the man who signs on the line.

It was all a disaster. Remember the Maine had worked very well.
Remember the names of the wounded,

the dead have plenty of sounds in their throats.
Scratched call letters on the back of a plane. Plane lands safe

under black cover or gets sacrificed to the chop
between us and Cuba.

Between the red
and the red white and blue.

I HAVE ANGER TOO

There's nothing in your hands.
I don't know what I was looking for, prying

at your thumb like that and how you let me wonder
and how you let me hurt you like that, your thumb bent back,

then fingers, palm, nothing in them. We search for the bullet,
shell casings, kin to the French Gunman Grassy Knoll.

The car got bought; it's in Dearborn.

A man stands at a bus stop popping his muscle
into a young girl's face. A woman looks up from her paper.

A boy rides his bicycle into the street, heavy traffic,
is not flattened the way you—reader—

expect him to be. It's fine.
He's fine. Everything's fine. He'll cross again,

this time at the light, right, like he's supposed to.
Some time he'll go into the woods and do something you don't want to hear
about.

For now he rides into his driveway, sets his bike against his father's car.
He might scratch the paint, he might get into trouble. But there's hurry here.

His mother, in the kitchen or dead on the stairs, pays him no mind.
In his room he finds his rifle. Then he points it at you.

(2)

THE PERFECT CONCUSSION
             MK-ULTRA

Watch as the man approaches the window,
his arms threaded in harm's departure.   Watch

as he weaves a flight suit out of bed sheets
and looks to the bad art over the bed for a message to move on.
                                        Oh god in heaven,

Harold be thy name.

                        Years later they'll say it wasn't his fault,
      what did he know,

                              shot in the arm with the blood of voodoo.

Involuntary cataclysm, Project Chatter, the runway.
                              Project Bluebird, Artichoke

and Church Committee.

      Digraph MK, man lost to the ULTRA.
                                    Stab

lines of conditioning, a gun in his hand, a gun to his head.
                                        Knockout pill,

to withstand privation,
      scars to the hands to the wall.

May produce amnesia
      (or talking out loud).
                              Winter waits for a walk
                                    through a tape loop of noise.

STOP TO THINK
Peak Oil

In another time I might try you—
on for tomorrow,
on for size.

We went over it again,
gave blood,
in,
peace a chance,
a damn,
it up.
Gave at the office.

I went all out,
all in,
and fell over again.
I drank it up,
him in, drank to war, 12-
stepped to fame. Dry
and high.
I'm sorry you didn't get the message.

We were old yesterday.
Told.
Today we learn to walk again.
In spring we can forget in God We Trust.
In-a-gadda-da-vida.
The green goes up, numbers
go down.
And people drive more.

The weather,
the warning.
Warming.
Living out is in again.
I'm not sure what to wear.

FORT LIVING ROOM
    Black Helicopters

A woman in a red dress as beacon. Rose against
a white wall, black against night, against the noise that keeps her up,
black crouches by the window and watches war.

The next day the helicopters will come. We won't see them until they are on us.
If a helicopter shadow passes before the hammer of engine and hurried blades,
then it is too late for turning children into wolves.

A crow will protect its nest from anything: shadows, a red dress.
I once thought only the crazy would survive war.
The crow in the tall tree in my yard leaves plums on my doorstep.

Sometimes the fruit stays perfectly smooth.
Oblong, skin intact, edible but for beak marks' bruising.
Sometimes with skin ripped it looks like the heart of an animal that died scared.

LITTLE BIRD
Black Helicopters

Winter. Daddy in the war. Only mother's blood. Only in the pale pink kitchen, the winter sky of knife. Five. Daddy paid the price. Head in oven, head over head tumble down the stairs. Sky. She never learned how in the pink she becomes dislodged. There's a secret here. We're in it. There were two of you. The Hummer breaks. Beat box. They came for you. Summer waits inside. Stutter. Neighbor's blonde brick wall cultivates wicked snakes of ivy. Ivy wrecks the plaster. Three drops of blood seep through savage suburban dream. Mother watched the wall. Heard the call. Blades destroying sound and thought. The blood. Carrot carnage, sway of milk, rubbed out ivory, ivory love, black helicopter. Generosity of courage or forgetfulness, nothing remains but fog. Then a tree full of red that emerges when blackened noise begins to clear.

POWDER BLUE

Chemtrails

"That plane carries exactly forty-
seven passengers," you say.
I don't know how you know this
or why you're telling me,
then, "the government poisons all of us
while we stand and look at the sun."
Blue days are like this.
Like the threaded sky threaded,
I'm lost in the folds of your powder blue shirt.
The sun comes off it, happy in my eye.
"There's nothing unpleasant about you at all," I say.
And I believe it with all of the crisscrossing
white blue shades, immaculate patterns
writing scripture above us.
"You're not listening to me," you say.
The sound of water breaks
the air like a knife fight,
like your mouth when it bites.

BLUE STREAK IN PARALLEL PLAY
Chemtrails

The tea smells like a page, not a window,
or some other recommended escape.
Wet bag folds over the chipped cup lip.
We see welts in the windmill once the fogcloud decides,
                                    banks left.
Let-loose saw cuts weathered for weeks
in the shape of a candle, or a jellyfish,
something that melts in the sun.

Pop goes the ring around rosy
fingers, pop goes the summertime.
What pleasantness swims to the shore,
moves without will on the waveline,
                            gets lost in the
sun, blocked by the wall of the upsurge,
that trembling canto.

What a memory of treeswell, the pile-high,
                            the wheel-
well making a ruckus with secreted things
shook loose from travel.

We'll get caught soon, lost,
                we'll unravel.

Your father went to jail for less than this,
    your father washed down with the   what.
Went mad for cough drops,
        a fancy car, a roof
through which his kids   could stare down the blue.

SKY SHIELD IS JUST VERTICAL WIND SHEAR & HUMIDITY

HAARP

I light a stack of beach grass I've stuck in the sand
and watch your face as winter waves wash the grey wind over you.

Contrails rest from red to pink, contrast extraordinary.
You're looking at pictures of your father again. No—

you're looking at barium, aluminum salts, thorium, silicon.
What got into your mother's head turned water to ice and polymer fiber.

We wait in the sharp grass for another cloud to form in the face
of your father. The snake of your bracelet slides over my hand.

Sand covers us after a time, warming. The planet is gathering heat.
It's said the Air Force will own the weather by 2025.

The purpose of chemical release is not global
dimming or population control. Then in the crisscross

and hashmarked sky, you see the baseball game where your father caught
the last foul ball, shape of his glove, shape of his horn, prisms

of light like the rest of us, like a papercut
redding the edge of your palm.

TOUGH PAPER AND 49 STICKS

Area 51

Mid-air collision no one saw,
but after. Two aircraft.
One in pieces, one nearly whole.
Four short bodies, ambulance—
three, three-and-a-half feet tall.

Flatbed truck, troops collect shards.
Like picking up sticks.

Hangar 84, Ohio airfield. Ohio wants to be shore.
51 is just a number.
Rocket launch to guide,
1945. Atomic research, rescuers, weather balloons.
The 509th bomb squad or Project Mogul.

What sets us apart
is our believing.
What sets us right, indecision,
that massive storm.

The I-beams, testing range.
What we would do with what we can't tear apart.
Fire in the sky, the sound in wind.
White sand, wet in flowers.
White writing on the wall.

FDR GETS UP FROM THE TABLE WITH HIS HANDS OVER HIS EARS

Pearl Harbor

When I heard "break squelch" I thought "smear the queer."
The games the boys would play.

Admiral stared across the water, never played hopscotch as a boy, never played cricket.
Air dense with cloud from water to endless.

Did you know he would do this? my mother asked, handling the officer's card.
Three broken windows in the bitch's yellow house. He never learned to play nice.

Sunset over the Pacific, but we were riding out of it.
The days grew shorter with speed.

Cards in a footlocker, 51, plus jokers.
Sailor searched the floor for that diamond four, not worth much, but still.

What did they know
and when did they know it?

My brother drew a picture of her severed head.
We didn't tell the cops.

Frank rolled back. Said he didn't want to know.
Or did he? Evidence shows we could decipher code.

Evidence shows we couldn't. End
the war. My brother put his fist through his bedroom wall.

MARKSMAN
MK-ULTRA

The war meant nothing to me, except what I couldn't avoid on TV.
Heat cake in the desert, black forest, mouth full of plans,

arm shot with red, venom, then training—bigger, harder, united we—
changed the channel quick, but sometimes things got through—

this bomb, that flag, fake pregnant bellies blowing up cars,
mad children with sticks, dead children with guns.

My brother wasn't the same when he got back.
He didn't want to talk about it, which was fine by me,

but parts of him kept telling things: eyes startled
at loud sounds, one hand slept on the butt of a gun.

With the TV on he was always more interested in what was for sale.
The man on the corner shouting, *cryptonym, delta, buy me some lime!*

His girlfriend fell down the stairs. His girlfriend walked into the door.
His dog ran away. His fingers bled teeth, knuckles wept in heat.

After Anders came home in a box we weren't allowed to see,
my brother filled the walls with holes.

"Shadows," he said.

He shot every
one.

DAY AFTER, OVER LONDON

Pan Am Flight 103

The world could end tonight.
That's why I'm eating this piece of cake.
That's why I don't care who won
the game last night. That's why
I haven't gotten the mail.
Why I haven't called you back,
written my father,
or watched the news.

I did take a shower.
I have
put on my best dress,
my best shoes.
I am eating this piece of cake.
The first piece was for me,
the second
for the end of the world.

The ascent has me pressed into my seat,
smell of luggage
leather and imaginary fire.
The girl in front of me taps her foot,
drums the armrest, taps her foot.
The engine sound ropes shrill at the end of the wing
like something is trapped inside
fucking things up.

I look from flight attendant to flight attendant,
then passenger to passenger.

END OF THE WORLD

I search for the terror
of gravity, of fire,
machinery gone awry.
On the ground,
houses burn like winter
until winter blows them out.

INTO OUR OWN FOOTPRINT
9/11

Black dust covered everything.
Pots and pans were filled, the sill, the plants,   bookends.
The dream was the same, black dust over everything.

In our sleep we hear sirens. On the train we hear sirens.
On the street. In the car. On TV.
Sirens inside the screen, outside the screen.   Outside the
window.

I heard sirens under water in the pool at the Y.
I thought about the East River,
about bodies in it, the jumpers

and the ones tossed in,   pushed in.
I met a man once at the bottom of the drink
with eyes wide and ankles in concrete.

In the dream you are underwater,
you hear sirens, then explode into the nothing of sky,
sirens, 97th floor, 77th, 49th and then—
nothing.

Convex web of grey,
blue grey, the eager sky through the devastating dawn of smoke—
all that smoke.   It's clear you'll never see the sun again. Body

blocks the ray, shadow on a building burning down.
They say the war's behind this. You're the echo.
You're the hiccup,   yet all depends on you.

END OF THE WORLD

I'm not waiting up, but when I wake up
I want the sill and pans to be clean,
the bookshelves, blinds,   your empty chair.

I want you on your hands and knees.

SWELL

9/11 and Tsunami

You say don't talk like that to me,
palm over the phone to sniff,
stiff little lip in the pre-dawn.
I set the coffee down,
will drink for both of us
until rage returns to silence.
Until I kiss you.
I know it's your mother
or your husband.
No one else gets your back up
so tall. The wall of water
came five years ago.
The mistress washed away.
Or the woman you thought was—
it doesn't matter now.
Not that stone had grown inside her.
Or the small hand
held
while hills receded
with a wash of hair
and mud
and timber.

GOING TO GROUND
Black Helicopter

We are alone for days in the heat of the hangar,
in the heat of the dark hotel.
We wait in the crawl space
for the black bladesound to deaden.
Steamed in fear and dust and noise.
Muffled by floorboards,
oak, bare and undone.

In my mind on hands and knees, strong
scent of linseed oil and lemon.
We're hung.
Finishing nails line the dirt,
pricking our knees.
House shaking, man-made earthquake firing the sky.

In a bar a few days after,
last bolt latched, knit tight on smoothblack wings.
Fingered in a pocket, plans to buy some land.
Someone said racehorse or mentioned *the customer*
and got the lobe of an ear bitten off.

What a man gets for being focused
on the sarcocarp, the slough, smooth, end of the line.
The British think it's us there,
waiting still. Butter in the black water,
full magazine.

CODE NAME MAIN STREET
Black Helicopter

They wanted to tap the Cau River line outside of Vinh.

That night the *quiet one* refueled at the Laotian border.

There were otters there and men with strange braces on their legs and faces.

And then the men with burns. Women

were ruined too, but none of them had names.

Nothing we could call them.

For months before flight a dozen men worked

to silence rotors, counter vortex formation, quiet air intakes.

Tiny tornadoes explode into ears.

Everything depends on hushed breath

and the static of fiber optics turning

into something translatable.

07:21:54 CAMERA 14

7/7 London Tube Bombing

What can be said about the photograph? Still
video from tube station, CCTV, men in motion,
black bags heavy in the neon storm,
that morning commute.
One bag sleeker,
man's midlife crisis
at 21. Eyes strain and blur at the harm
of pixelation, at the laziness of doctoring.
Yes, I see him. And yes,
you, with flowers in your hair, calendula, star-
gazer lily, nasturtium, daisy, sweet
William, sweet pea.
Yes, a good line is like lamplight.
I see where the blaze got in.
Luminosity, incandescent,
fulgor, flare, and splendor.
Rod of reflection through a young man's arm.
Through the side of a face,
beneath a white ball cap.
Cheek mimics sideways silo of handrail in false
color, in black and white.
Then the questions of time.
But what's a man supposed to do so superimposed?
Luton to King's Cross, Thameslink.
King's Cross to Tavistock Square
where the red bus rattled. Yes,
petals in your hair, dear.
Waxen mess on a cellar floor,
bathroom tile a mess, best

dressed in white
what with powder.
Spray paint never died so fine.
Paper, talcum, hands on frames,
chapatti flour and hair bleach
mixed in the bath at a flat in Leeds.

GREEN HOUSE
Peak Oil

Your mother stands on the balcony not saying anything.
Word has it she threatened to jump,
but now the pale rectangle of her exposed throat rises away from us,
in it her tongue and its strange silence.
"Mother," you say. But she says nothing.
Her hair waves and you want to take this as a sign,
but don't doubt the wind's indifference.
Your brother left home at the age of sixteen.
In his bedroom you found the diary that talked up the sea,
sand in all his shoes. Your mother gets up on the chair
that she placed between pots of geranium, pots of lilac,
lily. She's never even seen the ocean.
In the garage the car runs. In the garage the exhaust
heats up the roof with its black.

RINSE (AND OXIDATION)

Fluoride

On the ceiling I stared at the alphabet or whale, depending on the chair.
My teeth belonged to someone else.

There was machinery and I was lost to its buzzing and mint smell. I was lost
to the courtship of gloved fingernails snaking towards the back of my throat.

When I was five, mother monster stopped holding my hand.
She was like this in everything. At eight, church became choice

and we never heard bells again, became agents of the devil.
What the doctor said was good for us was never questioned.

The tumors grew and we around them, licking at dust on grandmother's Bible
and listening to the ache of errs our mouths had become.

SKYBUSTERS TRIGGERING TINY SIGNALS
HAARP

Your grandmother's land is choked in kudzu.
"I wish we could eat the stuff" she said. Green choked

tree cuts the sky in two. No more planes are out.
I wrote your name in the palm of my hand

not to forget you in the wake of mind control
the weathermen predict. When the clouds wash in

and the barometer drops I get a headache,
but what we're fearing is worse. Outside Gakona,

Saint Elias builds a shield made of light, spinning jenny.
A dervish. Whirling dead men play

strings that leave the heavens, the killing fields forty miles above us.
Touch the sweat on my face and the future shoots straight through you.

Electrical, my love. We live in the toaster; we wait for the bath.

HISTORY OF MIGRATION
7/7 London Tube Bombing

There is nothing deceiving about the Canadian grey goose.
A woman drags a child by a hot pink arm.

With wingspans of up to seven feet,
they carry summer-plumped bodies south in vees.

Don't you want to walk, the mother says.
Fourteen oblong specks in a green-grey sky.

Fourteen wingspans washing over downtown's bad pottery
of office stalls and migrant whispers.

A man's hand skirts the railing of basement stairs.

The child has stopped to look at the sky thinking,
mother can grant me this little *this*.

Stretched out sleeve in relief against
the faded paint of a painted brick wall where

graffiti once read "Time"
and a man was shot to death—

with a bullet in his hip
and a bullet in his brain.

THOMAS JEFFERSON & THE HOLY GRAIL

500,000 Plastic Coffins in Georgia

He says astrogeography. But ask if she's seen the sea.
Did the guys who guided the prisoners know?

Concentration camp under three feet of snow. Box
hammers unhooded heads in a dance.

Rampant outbreak. A tantrum
of outtakes. An osprey, my lamplight.

Birds culled, called
concentric intervening, like Dixie

cups, Alex Jones, perestroika, like Matryoshka dolls
underground. Mud

brick and mortar seams.
Nothing but the birds get through,

in nothing but dreams, in nothing but foot-
steps. Rat-a-tat tat. The girls upstairs intoxicated

on fat. Wig strands read on their hands
and coffee grounds in skull and

crossbone shapes at the bottom of mugs. Together
under the stairs, under the stars

together in this field in Georgia. We're close
enough to the airport to read numbers on the bellies

of low-flying planes. Close enough
to see our arms reflected,

lifting up to praise the racket
and what comes next in caskets,

nose against black plastic.

BELOW THE VAN ALLEN BELT
Lunar Landing

I want to live in a world where some things are broken,
but not the only things, not the good things that keep us
going. I want a fire where the only ones who get out
are the ones who were meant to burn.

Arsonists are such failures at love.
I have matches for fingers and I can strike them
anywhere. Yes, they're that kind of finger.
The bottom of a gumshoe's foot has seen

the palm of my hand. Then the slap.
When I slapped you it was hard
not to trace some part of you with my
sulfur tips. It's not true I'm the devil,

but I lit you up. You said you could see
yourself in my eyes—and not just that once—
you were on fire. I wanted to take care of you,
but history wouldn't let me. The stand of trees

where they found the body wouldn't let me.
The rough skin of your cheek—also called scar—
wouldn't let me. No blast crater under rocket fire,
ten thousand pounds of thrust. And how

could I trust you? I drove pictures of you to the ocean.
Men were fishing off the pier. There were kids there, but
no one was smiling. I heard the waves and the gulls and all of it,
everything you hear when you're there, which you weren't.

You were dead. Eight days of radiation.
The pier's boards were old, grey, nearly
worthless like most old grey things. I thought
someone should paint them, then remembered

how long it took us to weather the fence.
Sweet little pickets lining our yard.
I said we should do one section a week,
but that wasn't enough. You wanted to do all of it

at once. So I painted my section and you,
you finished the rest. You didn't come in for a week.
Cursed our biggish front yard. Cursed our palm trees.
If you can't make it, fake it. We were Floridians then

and we hated our lives. We didn't really have palm trees.
We didn't really have a house or a fence.
But the lives we were looking for, we painted them.
White paint over everything black, which was everything.

Then the pier, where I was and your pictures.
Eight days, weightless. And you know what I did.
I dropped them, some of them straight down,
some of them I ripped. There wasn't much wind.

You may have washed up on shore
or taunted surfers. You were diseased.
There was nothing to help you. If I'd had your ashes
I would have tossed those, but your memory burned instead.

And the scars that I gave you and the way you hid things under the stairs,
under the stars. I erased all of it, walking over those grey boards.
Walking past all those fishermen who probably weren't fishermen,
but men without work looking for something useful to do.

END OF THE WORLD

IMAGE SEQUENCE
9/11

Here is a vertical plane, two, sky,
the sky's the limit, less
shipping, nightshade, handling.

Smell of fetish and feel of corn silk.
The man on the train looked at you
strange. We were up all night stuffing

envelopes for the 34th floor.
There's no one there, nothing
but cheap carpet and industrial

lighting, nothing but white
ceiling tiles, white walls.
Boxes move like animals we don't see.

When we get more specific they turn
into bears, fiery, immobile growlers wheeled
across vacant skyline. History of rails.

For 49 hours all the planes stopped.
White jet leaning towards infamy,
the president's roar. Bells to keep him wilder.

Silent children leaning
on knees toward the trusted animal.
There's nothing there but scare and fur.

We waited 14 hours and no one came.
We gave blood like hearts could leave veins.
We came to give it all. And take it.

Thirty thousand anthills blooming
in overhead bins. Tired of tracking movement,
I chase your blip from the screen.

Wind caught an enemy. There was a power
down, a power out. We put up with no lights, no fire,
the end was near.

The phones won't work, windows break and paper
shoots out through scars in the hull.
God knows we loved it all.

I retouched my makeup,
you let down your hair.
Timeline is a lazy lover's zipper.

We were never there.
I wanted to stay late, but the building shut down.
Seismic rocks before the first contact.

But then the sign gets in. Free coffee for everyone
from the top to ground floor.
We had it all and we knew it was something,

but we were thinking moustache,
man on the train, the first embrace,
the start before leaving, fist

around a tie, foot on the bedroom door,
the last embrace, hot hand slides over telephone;
you were only joking.

You're only joking now.
An empty pit. That's not the end of this.
The war and all that chocolate, fear.

The paper cuts. We wore each other's clothes.
We wintered, wanted. You can't have
loved me. My picture's on a wall.

OPEN SHOWN IN WHITE

500,000 Plastic Coffins in Georgia

There was sweat against the pylon, wet.
The way we moved there, night.
To follow night. Light against the treetrunk split the house
in two.   I never loved you.

I found a thousand red ants inside my car.
Under the hood, industrious. Two moved
tightly across tiny wires.
The crack in plastic big enough, just.
I tapped the hard black box and.
Out they swam. Dark
clay shattered. Red smoke thick
with sunbeam night wanted to fight.

I am not me again
here, bright light against the headbeam,
smashed. I am   *That* girl
in 1999 staring at the future's lip,
which is also the lip of some fine girl,
pressed to red.
The century will start two years later like some weird
motor, some bleary horn we're on.

Were those who bought tickets moving
any faster than the dock departing?
Cuts of glass, her hand across
your shoulder meant you
were going nowhere,

END OF THE WORLD

at the speed of heat.
Night becomes day again, night—
cycle tightens. Thirteen forks stuck
in thirteen rabid animals. A to the—
a horrent horizon darts redly down the road.

Out there the lane lines lie
covered in glass from another animal
accident. They didn't see
when the husky crossed the road.
Ditch lined up to meet them, man, beast,
head to glorious ditch.

WAITING UP FOR THE END OF THE WORLD

This one's a love poem. This
is how we burn. So what, we're speeding up

the way the world will end, let's make it
beautiful. Let's make it ours.

Without snow there are no ski slopes,
only hills without injury.

No melting ice pack. Nothing to slip
on, we bump one another, frailty to

frailty, slick against GDP, faster father, sick
against the pale wet side of the road.

I look for a place in with everyone.
Your tiny lungs are not my fault. Your tiny brain.

The ship is mine and it's sinking.
You are not what you were

just a moment ago. Two tall-ish giraffes—not
the biggest ones—and a bucketful of gay,

inconsiderate swans. Rostrum and ritual
linens, bleach smell that won't fade.

We stuff the hole with burlap sacks,
we stuff the hole with holes.

END OF THE WORLD

Tongue, the agent of speech and love. In
words we reproduce. My open mouth

against your open mouth against
the odds, the warming, sea rise.

There's nothing spectacular about the way we pin
each other down, the way we waste the day.

This is the way we walk to the bank,
and how we live with ourselves.

(0)

TO KEEP A BODY FAITHFUL

What you said is true again, history rises
or circles back to meet us, again,   again.
Like wild dogs padding down grass
or bad manners ruining banquets.
What gets done is not the same as what's done
to us.   Or is it?

I identify change by the satellites, by the words on TV,
or what were words become images.
Now that pictures
are king again.

Poppies at the side of the road burst into bloom.
Then, in a slow succession of green, a fade into syllables,
symbols. What night was, once. What timing.
What an age for dreams.   When winter breaks.
When the earth hollows out,
separates,   stills.

Acknowledgements

Special thanks to Andrea J. Danowski, Sheri Rysdam, and Francis McNairy, who make the world worth living in. Big thanks to Suzanne Paola and Amy Schrader, who read and helped shape this manuscript through nascent forms. Thanks to Bruce Beasley and Oliver de la Paz. And to Linda Bierds, Andrew Feld, Deborah Poe, Kate Lebo, Piper Daniels, Katherine Eulensen, Emily Sketch Haines, Thomas Martin Grout, Katie Hoffman, Luke Laubhan, Peter Moench, Calvin Pierce, Rich Smith, and Erika Wilder, Jay Yencich, who read and offered valuable insight to some of these poems. Thanks also to Debra Di Blasi and Sam Witt for their vision of the future, and including this book in it. Special thanks as always to Carol Guess, without whom this book could not have been written.

Additionally, I'd like to express great appreciation to the editors of the following journals and anthologies, in which some of these poems originally appeared:
Another Chicago Magazine: "Northwoods"
Anti—: "Motor of the World"
Barn Owl Review: "From Love Field"
BLIP: "Rinse (and Oxidation)"
A Face to Meet the Faces: An Anthology of Contemporary Persona Poetry: "The Woods Behind General Walker's House"
Front Porch Journal: "California Ice Age"
Gulf Stream: "November 22"
The Journal of Compressed Creative Arts: "Genesis"
Mandala Journal: "Fort Living Room", "Wise Men Poisoned the Well", "Marksman"
NOÖ Journal: "FDR Gets Up from the Table with His Hands Over His Ears"
Poets for Change: "American Fear"
Quiddity Literary Journal: "The Devil Wages Ordinary Wars"
Slant Poetry: "Green House," "MK-NAOMI," "The Perfect Concussion"
The Southern Poetry Anthology, Volume V: Georgia: "Little Bird"
350.org: "King Hubbert"
RHINO: "Toshiba Bombeat"
Whiskey Island: "The Mathematics Of"

Also:

"Rinse (and Oxidation)," "Fluoride is Fluorescent Incandescent" and "Home Before Dark, The Protocols Of" also appeared in chapbook *Dear Mother Monster, Dear Daughter Mistake* (Rose Metal Press, 2011) in considerably different form.

Poem "The Mathematics Of" appeared as a limited edition chapbook/broadside as part of Pace University's Handmade/Homemade exhibit, March 2011.

** "Toshiba Bombeat" is for First Officer, Raymond Ronald Wagner.

** Italicized lines in "07:21:54 Camera 14" — Reed, Sue. "Conspiracy fever: As rumours swell that the government staged 7/7, victims' relatives call for a proper inquiry." The Daily Mail. 3 July 2009. (http://www.dailymail.co.uk/news/article-1197419/Conspiracy-fever-As-rumours-swell-government-staged-7-7-victims-relatives-proper-inquiry.html#ixzz1S3R1hUQW)

**Title "To Keep a Body Faithful" comes from a line from Sophie Cabot Black's poem "The Stray"

**"The Devil Wages Ordinary Wars" was inspired by Jennifer Borges Foster

CONSPIRACY THEORIES, CAST OF
(IN ORDER OF APPEARANCE)

Fluoride

some people believe fluoride is put in public water sources not for health of teeth, but for mind control.

Pan Am Flight 103

some people believe Libya was framed.

Area 51

some people believe an alien spacecraft crashed at Roswell, NM in 1947 and that the government houses proof of this and other strange things at Area 51 in Nevada.

Lunar Landing

some people don't believe we went to the moon.

The Philadelphia Experiment

some people believe the USS Eldridge time traveled.

9/11

some people believe it was an inside job.

HAARP

some people believe the High Frequency Active Aural Research Program (HAARP) in Alaska is a weapon used to lift and/or tear whole sections of atmosphere in order to disrupt planes and missiles, cause earthquakes, and/or modify weather.

Pearl Harbor

some people believe the U.S. had prior knowledge of the attack.

The Protocols of Zion

some people still believe this discredited document is a how-to for world domination.

North American Union

some people believe Mexico, Canada, and the U.S. will unite to become the "NAU" as the next step in the New World Order.

Birthers

some people do not believe President Barack Obama was born in the U.S.

December 2004 Tsunami

some people believe this tsunami was manmade.

MK-ULTRA

some people do not believe the CIA ever discontinued this program of mind control and interrogation through chemical means.

7/7 London Tube Bombing

some people believe there was government involvement.

Chemtrails

some people believe some contrails left by planes contain the purposeful release of chemicals or biologic agents.

Princess Diana

some believe it was murder.

Black Helicopters

some people believe they have seen these unmarked signs of covert operation and harbinger of military takeover.

Peak Oil

some people believe we are not running out of oil, that saying so is a effort to continually inflate prices.

500,000 Plastic Coffins

some people believe these coffins located in a field in Georgia are part of an imminent plan including concentration camps and martial law.

About the Author

Elizabeth J. Colen was born in the Midwest, raised in the Northeast, has lived in the Southeast, and currently makes her home in the Pacific Northwest. Author of Lambda Literary Award nominated prose poetry collection, *Money for Sunsets* (Steel Toe Books, 2010) and flash fiction collection, *Dear Mother Monster, Dear Daughter Mistake* (Rose Metal Press, 2011), she also occasionally blogs about books, libraries, and train travel at http://elizabethjcolen.blogspot.com.

This book is also available as a
beautiful full color print edition
with original art
by Guy Benjamin Brookshire.

13636566R00077

Made in the USA
Charleston, SC
22 July 2012